DENTISTS TAKE CARE OF OUR MOUTHS

Grateful acknowledgment is made to
Dr. Sanford L. Barr, DDS, LTD.
Chicago, Illinois

Design and Art Direction
Lindaanne Donohoe Design

Library of Congress Cataloging-in-Publication Data

Greene, Carol.

Dentists take care of our mouths/by Carol Greene.
p. cm.
Summary: Describes the different kinds of work which dentists do
such as checking teeth and filling cavities. Questions and answers at
the end offer further information about this profession.
ISBN 1-56766-405-9 9 (lib. bdg.)
1. Dentist — Juvenile literature. 2. Dentistry — Juvenile literature.
[1. Dentists. 2. Dentistry. 3. Occupations.] I. Title.

RK63.G735   1997   97-835
617.6—dc21   CIP
                                                              AC

DENTISTS TAKE CARE OF OUR MOUTHS

By Carol Greene

Photographs by Phil Martin

THE CHILD'S WORLD®

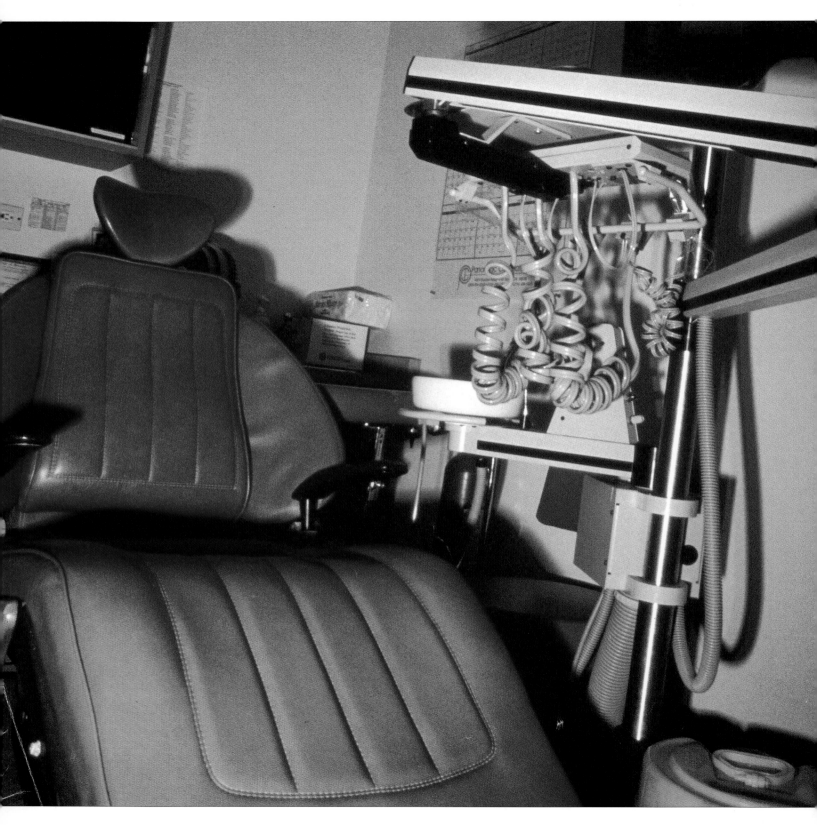

The dentist plays soft music in his office. He checks his tools. Everything is clean and ready for his first patient.

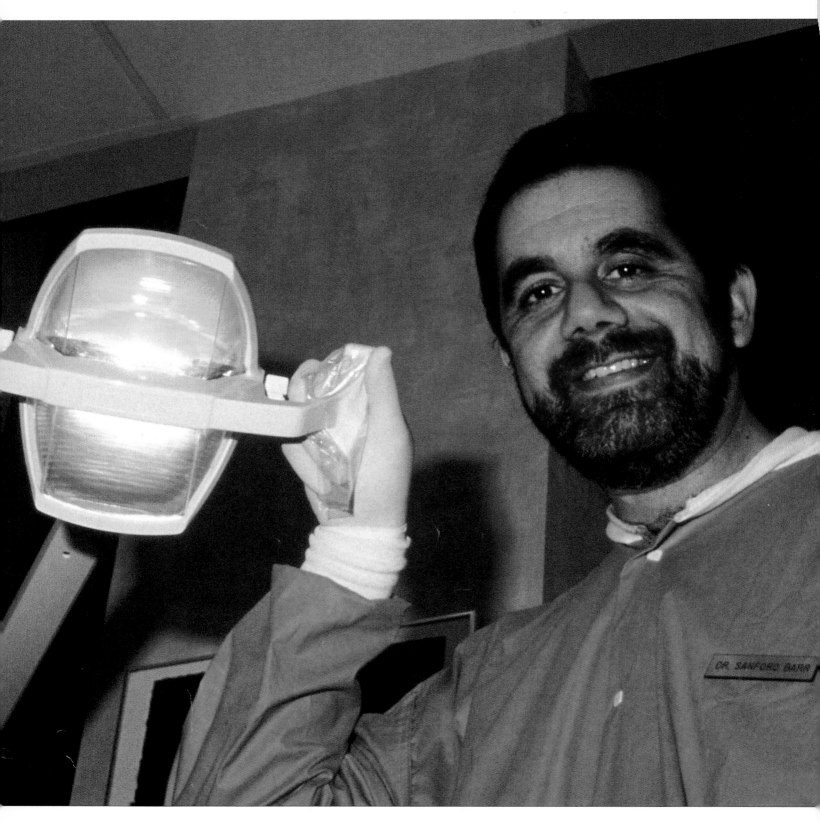

The dentist moves the chair up.

WHOOSH!

He turns on a bright light.

CLICK!

Now he can see everything.

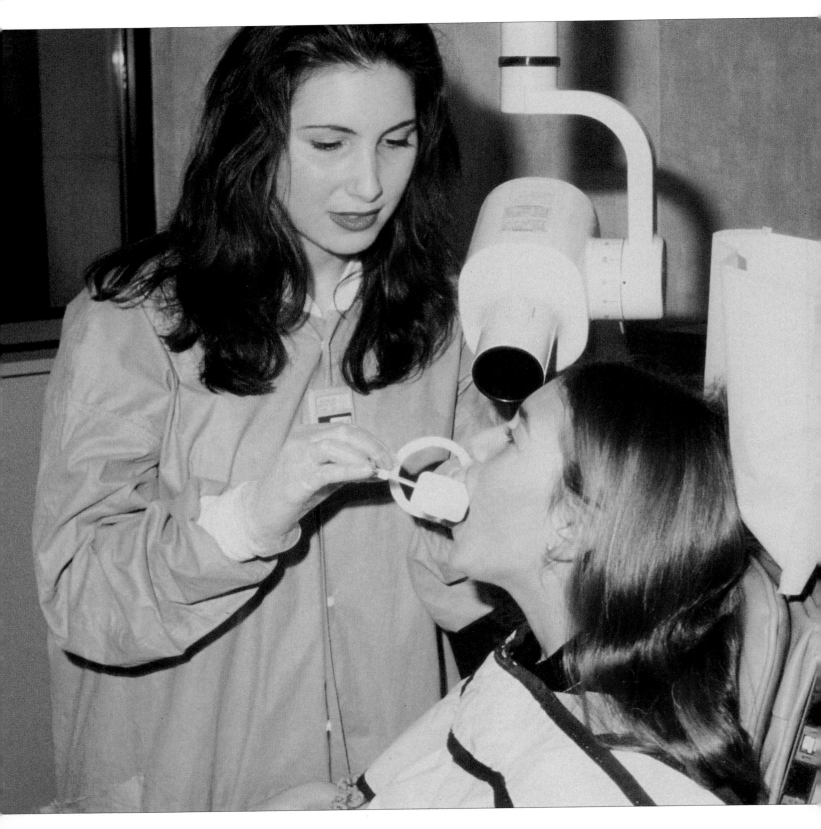

This girl has come for a checkup.

The dentist's helper uses an

x-ray machine to take pictures

of the girl's mouth.

BZZZT!

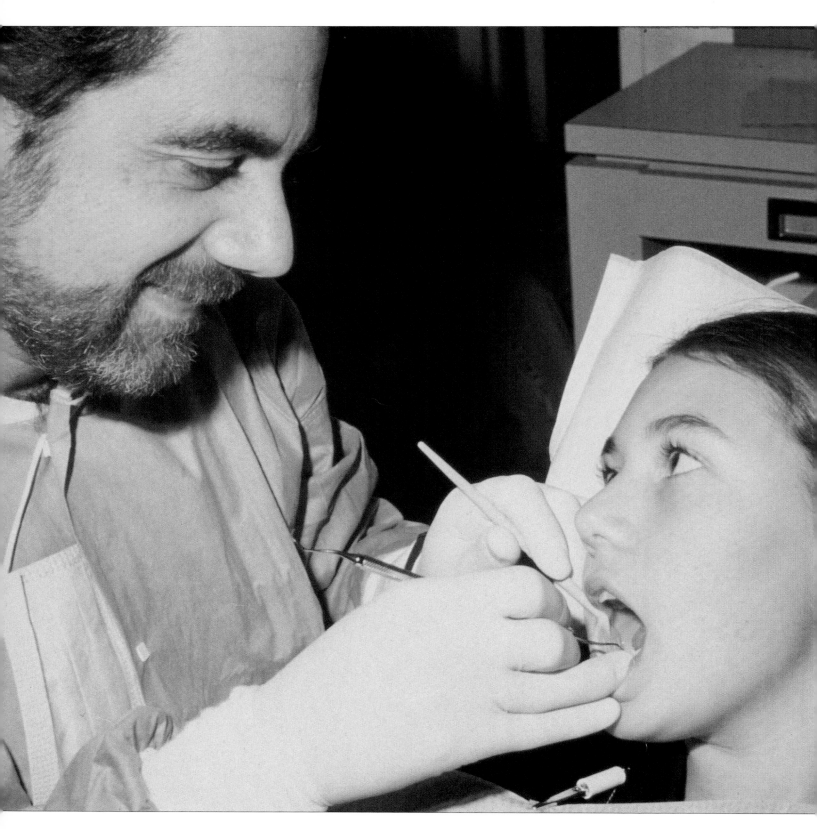

This girl needs her teeth cleaned.

The dentist uses a scaler to take

the tartar off her teeth.

SCRAPE! SCRAPE!

Tartar is a mix of germs and minerals.

It is bad for teeth.

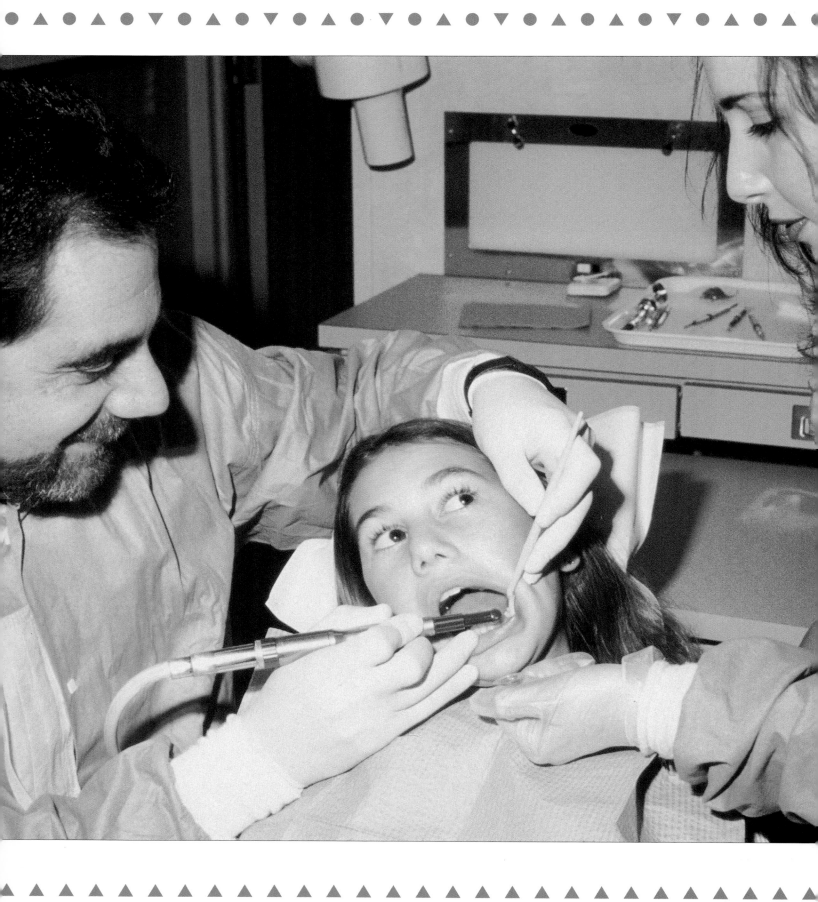

The dentist polishes the girl's teeth

with a polisher. *WHIRRR!*

"That tickled," says the girl.

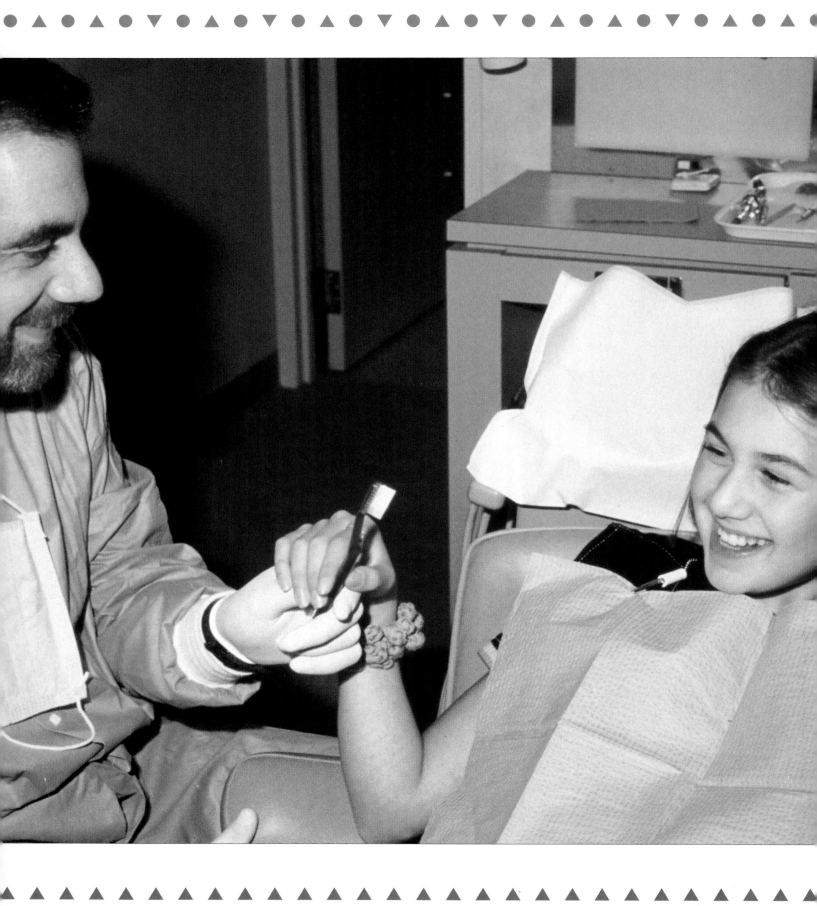

"Your teeth and gums are fine.

You have no cavities," says the dentist.

He gives her a new toothbrush.

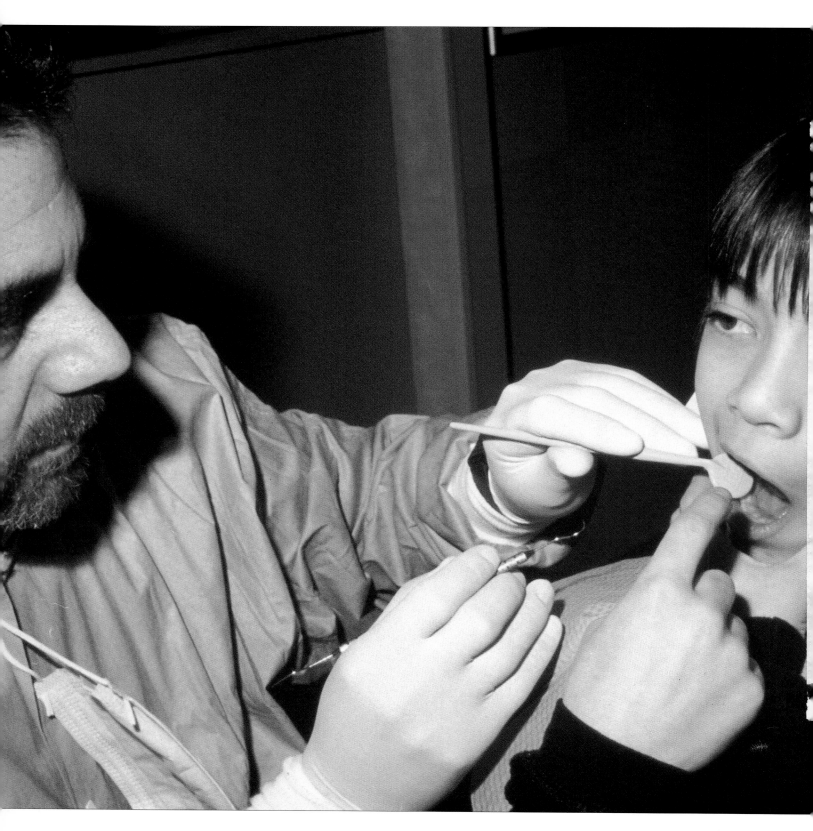

This boy has a toothache.

"OWWWW!" he says.

The dentist looks in his mouth.

"You have a cavity," he says.

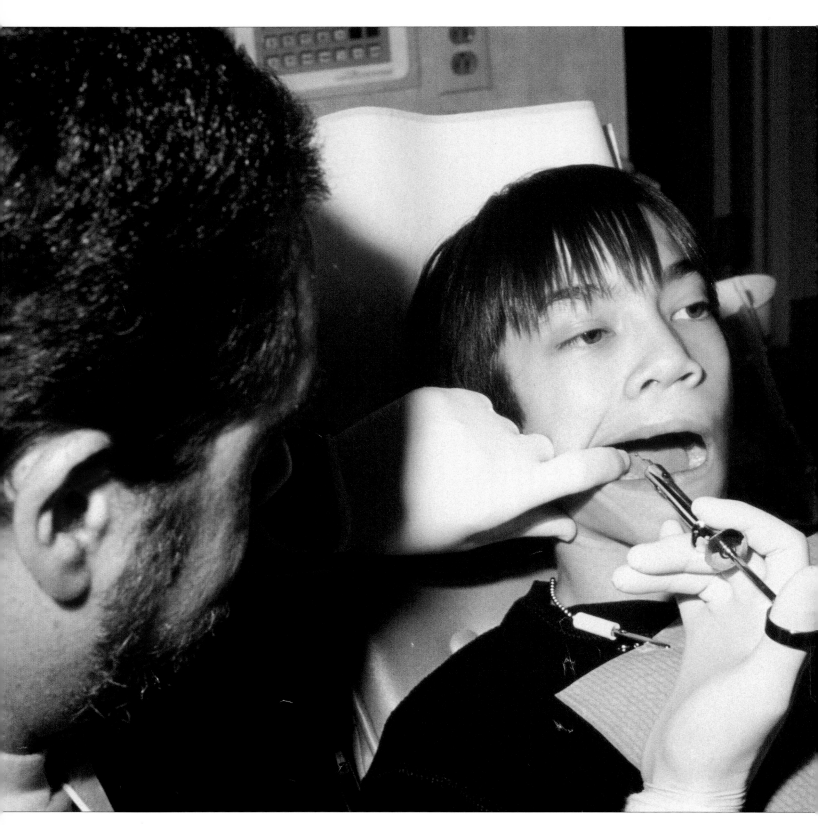

He gives the boy a shot.

ZAP!

Now the boy won't feel any pain when the dentist fixes his tooth.

BZZZZZ!

The dentist uses a tool called a burr.

It cuts away the bad parts of the tooth.

The dentist washes and dries the tooth.

SHHHHHH!

Then he puts a silver filling

into the tooth.

TAP-A-TAP-TAP!

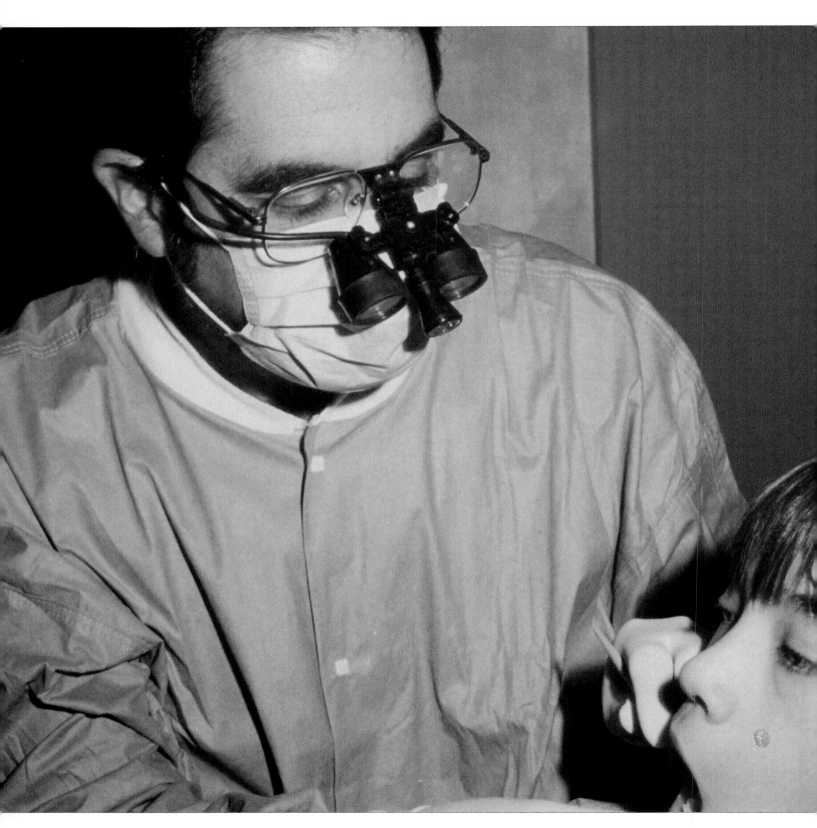

"Be sure to brush twice a day," says the dentist. "Use floss too. Flossing gets out food that sticks between your teeth. If tiny pieces of food are left in your mouth, they can cause cavities."

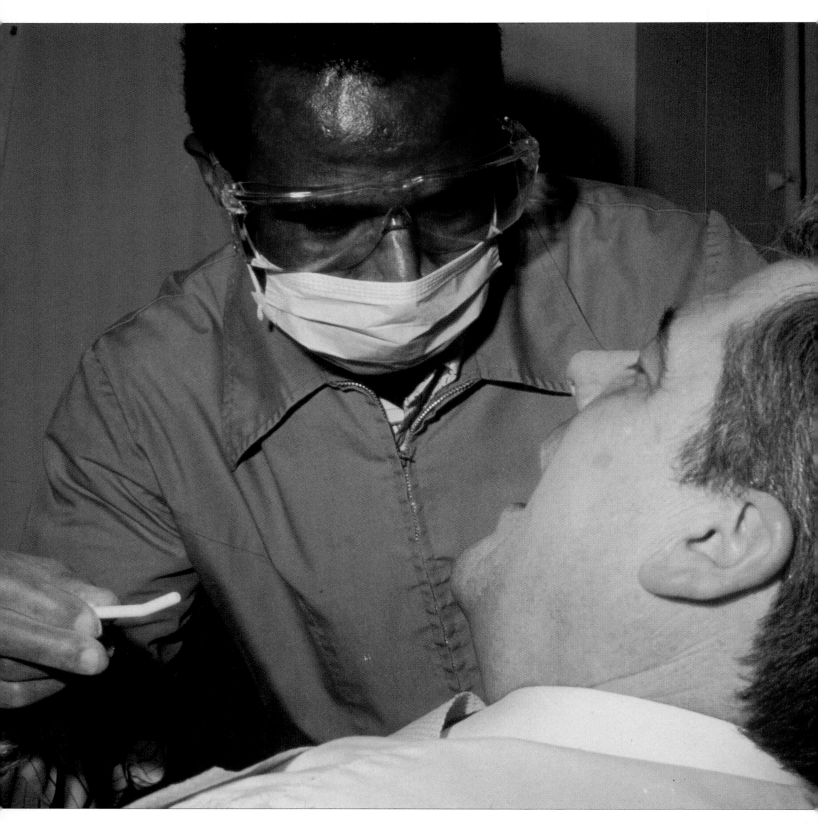

This man says,

"I am tired of having crooked teeth."

This dentist checks his teeth.

"Your teeth and gums are healthy,"

he says. "But straight teeth would make

you feel better and look better too.

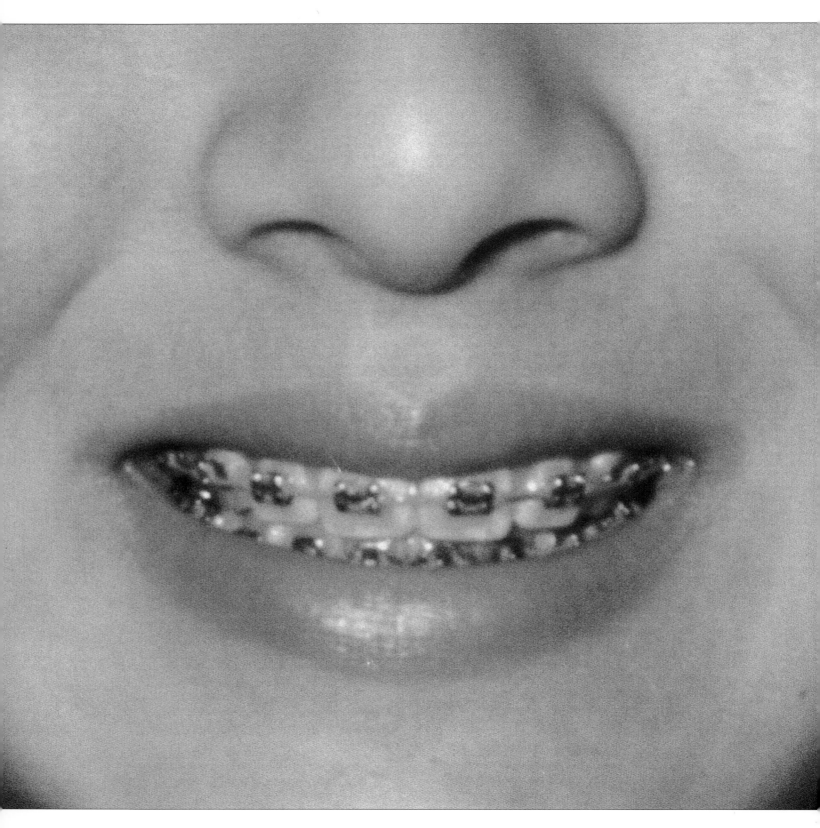

Braces will straighten your teeth.

Many of my patients wear them."

"Fine!" says the man.

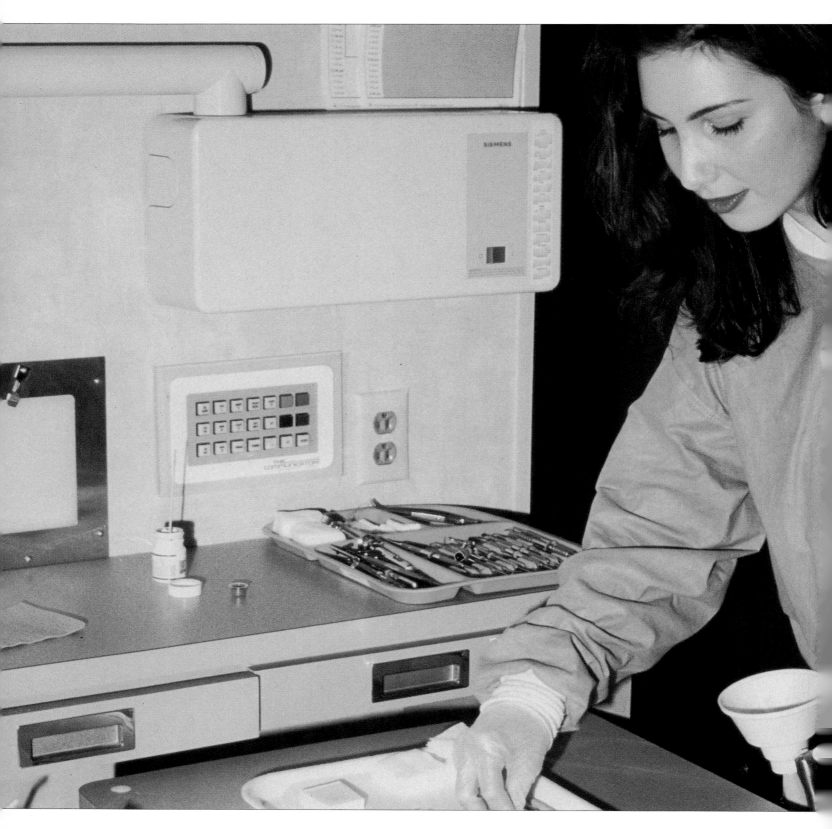

The morning is over.

The dentist's helper has many

instruments to clean.

CLINK!   FZZZZ!

Everything must be ready for the

afternoon patients.

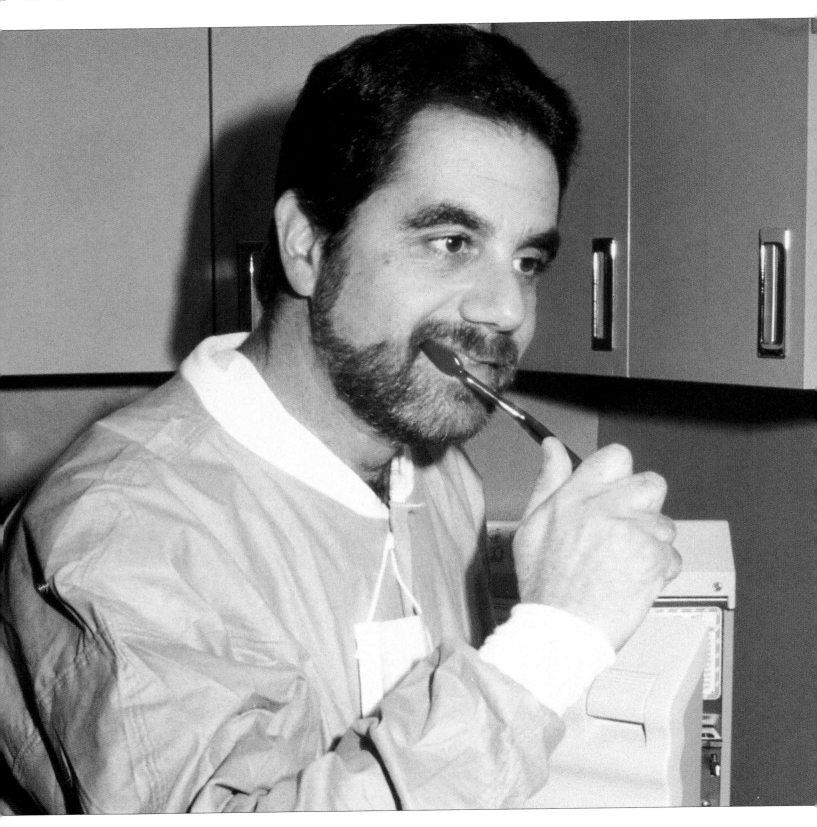

This dentist eats lunch at his desk.

Can you guess what he does next?

He brushes his teeth!

Questions and Answers

What do dentists do?

Dentists take care of our teeth and gums. They help us keep our mouths healthy. They fix diseased or injured teeth and gums. Some dentists do only one special job, such as giving people braces. Some work only with children. Others have patients of all ages.

How do people learn to be dentists?

Most dentists go to college for four years. Then they take a test. If they pass, they go to dental school for four more years. Here other dentists teach them how to fix teeth and how to help people keep their teeth and gums healthy. Then they must pass another test to get a license.

What kind of people are dentists?

Dentists must be smart and good at science. They must be able to do careful work with their hands. Dentists should like people and enjoy working with them.

How much money do dentists make?

Some dentists make more than $75,000 a year, but others make much less than that. How much a dentist makes, often depends on how many patients he or she sees each day.

About the author

Carol Green has written over 200 books for children. She also likes to read books, make teddy bears, work in her garden, and sing. Ms. Green lives in Webster Groves, Missouri.